Lawler Education — *Literacy Matters*

Skills for Literacy 4

Dr Susan Young

LAWLER EDUCATION

Skills for Literacy 4

Dr Susan Young

The author's rights have been asserted.

© 2018 GLMP Ltd All Rights Reserved.

978-1-84285-458-7

Series Editor: Dr Graham Lawler

Produced and Published by Lawler Education

Lawler Education
Lon Ffawydd/Beech Lane
Abergele
LL22 7DY
www.graham-lawler.com
Lawler Education is a division of GLMP Ltd
and is not affiliated, endorsed or sponsored by any external organisation.

Copyright Notice
The copyright of this book grants the right for one tutor at one provider site to photocopy the activities.
A Multi-User Licence must be purchased for each additional tutor using the same resource at the same site.
Additional Multi-User licences can be purchased at any time.
For providers with multiple sites, each site is treated as an independent site and the above paragraph applies.
The ongoing supply of these materials depends on tutors' professional good judgment and compliance with copyright law. This resource is covered by UK and European copyright law, and CLA polices its use.

You acknowledge in the use of this resource that you are applying your own professional judgement in determining the suitability of the goods for any particular purpose. Neither the publisher nor any/all of their agents can be held accountable for outcomes with students as a result of usng this resource. Teachers should review the resource in the light of their knowledge of their determination of the needs of their student.

Skills for Literacy 4

Number/General Thinking Series
Introducing Algebra 1: Number Patterns and Sequences
Introducing Algebra 2: Specialising and Generalising
Introducing Algebra 3: Introducing Equations
Introducing Algebra 4: Equations and Graphs
Number and Place Value
Entry Level: Writing and Forming Numbers

Aber Education Teacher Books
Family Relationships
Bullying and Conflict
Hey Thompson
Self-Esteem and Values
Self-Esteem: a Manual for Mentors
Enhancing Self-Esteem in the Adolescent
Grief, Illness and Other Issues
Survival Teen Island: The Ultimate Survival Guide for Teenagers

Emotional Well Being and Health
Choose Happiness
The Eat Well Stay Slim Budget Cookbook
Write Yourself Well

English
Creativity through Language 1: How to Teach Fictional Writing
Creativity through Language 2: How to Teach Informative/Non-Fictional writing

Cloze
Cloze: Cars and Transport

Year 3-4 Crosswords
More Year 3-4 Crosswords

Guided Reading and Writing
More Guided Reading and Writing

Reading for Comprehension 1
Reading for Comprehension 2
Reading for Comprehension 3
Reading for Comprehension 4

Skills for Life
More Skills for Life

Skills for Literacy 1
Skills for Literacy 2
Skills for Literacy 3
Skills for Literacy 4
Skills for Literacy 5
Skills for Literacy 6
Skills for Literacy 7
Skills for Literacy 8

Writing and Forming Letters

Writing in Everyday Life Book 1: Making Inferences
Writing in Everyday Life Book 2: Travelling
Writing in Everyday Life Book 3: Asking Questions
Writing in Everyday Life Book 4: Messages

Vital Phonics 1
Vital Phonics 2
Vital Phonics 3
Vital Phonics 4

History
Active Lives 1
Active Lives 2

Cross Curricular
Titanic: The Story of a Tragedy

Financial Literacy/Capability
Back to the Black for Primary Schools

www.graham-lawler.com

We wish to thank the author Edward G James for use of the John Mundela, Jack Caeser and Dax Brydon characters from his forthcoming crime series.

Many more titles in development

Teacher Feedback Opportunity

£20 Lawler Education Voucher for detailed and complete reviews. The purpose of this form is to give you, the teacher, an opportunity for improvement/positive feedback.

Resource Name_____ Resource ISBN_____

Your Name_____ Your Position_____

School Name_____

Address_____

_____

Overall, what do you think about this resource ?_____

_____

_____

How does it help your students ?_____

_____

_____

What could you say to a colleague in a neighbouring school to persuade them to use this resource ?

_____

_____

How well does it match the specification and which specification is it ?_____

_____

Other Comments, suggestions for improvement, errors, please give the page number

_____

Resources I would like published

_____

Resources I might like to write, or have written, for consideration for publishing.

_____

Fax: 01745 826606   email: info@graham-lawler.com
post: Lawler Education, Lon Ffawydd, Abergele LL22 7DY

Contents

Tutor Notes Session One	7
Worksheet 1	8
Worksheet 1b	9
Worksheet 2	10
Worksheet 3: More Tenses Practice	11
Worksheet 4: Even More Tenses Practice	12
Worksheet 5: Matching	13
Crossword 1	14
Tutor Notes Session 2	15
Worksheet 1	16
Worksheet 2	17
Worksheet 3	18
More on the Past progressive Form	19
Even More on the Past Progressive Form p20	20
Tutor Notes Session 3	21
Worksheet 1	22
Worksheet 2	23
Worksheet 3	24
Tutor Notes Session Four	25
Worksheet 1	26
Worksheet 2 More on Apostrophes	27
Worksheet 3 Even More on Apostrophes	28
Worksheet 4 Yet Even More on Apostrophes	29
Wordsearch	30
Answers	31-37
Interactive White Board Activities	38-39

Tutor Notes Session One

Starter
Work through worksheet 1 with the students. This is a warm up for students.

Main activity
Work through the slide show with the students asking them to find the inconsistencies with the tenses. If you can, show this on a smart board and ask volunteers to circle the inconsistent tenses.

This is slide one

The college cafeteria is usually very crowded but recently things **are** worse than usual. We had a visiting soccer team from London and the principal **inviting** them for lunch. An extra twenty people is not a lot in a large hall but when you are in a crowded cafeteria something will give and it did. The partition separating the cafeteria from the staff area collapsed. We **have** college teachers looking at students. Dr Lawson **is** very unhappy as he was hit by the falling partition.

Now ask the students to work through worksheet 1b

Plenary
Ask them to work through session one worksheet 2. Students may be interested to know that Edward G James is a real author and currently writes for Lawler Education and Hamilton-Vale Publishing and is planning a crime series featuring Detective Inspector Mundela.

The other worksheets for this session require your professional judgement.

Session One Worksheet 1   Name ....

Using the Verb 'To be'.

Write the correct form of the verb ' to be' in the present tense.

    She   He   We   It   They

Example: I (be) **am** happy.   **Example:** We/They/You (be) **are** happy.

1) I (be) _____ hungry.   2) I (be) _____ late.

3) I (be) _____ happy.   4) I (be) _____ tired.

5) We (be) _____ early.   6) We (be) _____ busy.

Example: He/She/ It (be) is late.

7) He (be) _____ interesting.   8) She (be) _____ fun.

Now we'll use nouns instead of pronouns.

9) Kevin (be) _____ happy.   10) Sally and Claire (be) _____ my friends.

11) Nisha (be) _____ watching tv.   12) The hammer drill (be) ____ new.

13) The students (be) _____ laughing.   14) The test (be) _____ hard.

15) Manisha (be) _____ cooking dinner.

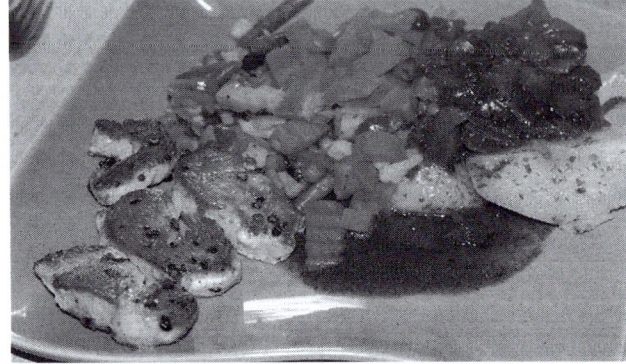

Session One Worksheet 1b   Name..............................

Add words in the paragraphs to make sure it all makes sense.

Aiko .... starting a job in London next week. She......... be working for a major media company. Her job involves meeting clients and designing adverts .... on the radio. She .... to learn a lot about British commercial radio because it .... is so different to the radio she .... used to back in Japan. Living .... London is exciting for young people because there .... so much happening. London .... top premier football teams and great West End shows, wow life .... exciting.

Kiku .... a student at Derwen College until last year.
Then she left .... become a trainee manager at a gardening nursery. She .... now studying management as part of her training. She hopes,........the future, to study for a high management qualification called an M.B.A. Kiku said, ' If I .... part-time and .... part-time I can combine the best of both worlds.' The future .... going to be hard .... but ..... will be exciting!'

Jayne .... delighted to receive her three puppies from her husband. The puppies were to mark thirty years of marriage. Jayne said ' my husband Jacob thought it would be nice to have a pup for each decade'. Jayne ...... Jacob by chance, when they both worked for a large health company. They .... both dentists and both .... for the same dental practice in Chester.
The puppies .... looked after during the day by a kennel maid who ...., ... and .... with them so they .... content. Even so, every night when Jayne and Jacob .... home from work, the puppies are so .... to see them and run around like crazy for about ten minutes. It .... great that they are so happy!

Cathy and Jim .... a new kind of worker. They .... called ' digital nomads'. That means they work on laptops and .... work from anywhere in the world. This .... great for young people because it means they .... provide services online that someone else, anywhere else, ... buy. Cathy and Jim write code, and .... can work anywhere where there......... access to the internet.
They have both .... a lot and .... visited a lot of countries; what a fantastic life!

© 2018 Lawler Education Teachers may copy these pages for use in their own school.

Session One Worksheet 2   **Name**..................................

Complete the gaps in the following story.

Choose from the words below, you may use some words more than once.

entertain, is, has, means, opened, part, is, police, make, writes, question,

means, working, writing, Dax, happen, turned, been, author, reader, book,

books, puzzles, cop, popular, read, accurate, started, walked, move, ask

Detective Inspector John Mundela……. a secret. By day he …. a hard working police officer in Chester but at night he ….. a different job. John Mundela had developed a new ……..-time lucrative career as a novelist. This………. he writes books to …………. his readers.

The real point ….. that none of his fellow workers know that he …..the famous novelist Dax Brydon. Lots of other ……officers have commented on how realistic the ….. Brydon stories are but no-one has ever thought to……… who writes them and John Mundela has never said.

He …………under a pseudonym. This ….. a false name and it ………. he can have a private life and make money but why does he carry on ……….. as a police officer ?

The real reason is that ……….. novels is not that well paid. People do it for the love of it and if they ………….to make a lot of money well that is great but the vast majority simply do not ………. a great deal of money.

This has never ……… a problem for Mundela. He enjoys the ……….. process of making a novel, the most. Plotting means working out 'whodunnit' or who …..the killer. Then the …….has to lay a series of clues in the story to tempt the reader and the game is that the ………….has to try and work it out before the end of the………… Millions of people love ……….like this, not because they are gruesome stories of murder but because they are ………. and who does not like a good puzzle ? This is also the reason that there are so many ………. shows on tv.

Mundela's detective ….. called Jack Caeser. This …. a great name for a cop and one that has proven to be very ……with the public. His last novel was called Caeser's Palace and was set in the police station in Chester. People who ……….. the book were amazed at how ………………the descriptions were but they simply did not realise that the author was ………… in the building most days of the week.

Mundela ……….writing, ' The door handle ……… and the door ……….. slowly. Detective Inspector Jack Caeser ………. into the room.'

Session One Worksheet 3
More Tenses Practice

Name..

Complete the following sentences using the correct tense form.

1. My sister _____ the dog for a walk every afternoon.

   took, takes, is taking

___

2. We are _____ to Chester tomorrow.

   gone, been, going

___

3. Jan was _____ to see Graham after so many years, they were friends in college.

   pleasing, pleased, please

___

4. We _____ here for twelve years.

   are living, have lived, have living, live

___

5. Mark _____ his lunch in the staff restaurant when I saw him.

   is having, has had, was having, has

___

6. We _____ her before.

   never saw, are never seeing, have never seen, seen

___

7. I _____ the solicitor last week.

   are meeting, have met, met, have meeting

___

8. She said she will _____ you tomorrow

   have seen, see, seen, saw

Session One Worksheet 4
Even More Tenses Practice

Name..

Mark and Sarah were _____ (drive) along the M6 to visit friends in the midlands when they realised they needed to stop for petrol. They _____ (stop) at a service station and everything _____ (seem) fine. Mark was _____ (fill) the car when he _____ (hear) a noise. He _____ (see) two masked men with guns _____ (surround) a security van that had _____ (arrive) to collect the money from the petrol station.

Mark left the petrol pump holster in the tank and _____ (creep) along the side of the car to the passenger door. He _____ (says) to Sarah 'slide down onto the floor and stay there'. Sarah just _____ (nod). She was very _____ (fright) and was not going to argue. Mark then _____ (hide) behind the petrol pump and got his phone.

He _____ (dial) 999 but when the operator _____ (answer), he couldn't _____ (say). So he waited and then _____(press) 55. This is a way of _____ (tell) the operator that to speak or make a noise is _____ (danger). Thankfully after about 5 minutes police cars _____ (arrive) and the criminals were _____ (arrest). Mark and Sarah _____ (give) their details to the police and were soon on their way. Their friends were _____ (amaze) when they _____ (hear) what _____ (happen).

Session One Worksheet Five
Matching

Name..................................

In the PAST column write down the past tense of the word in the PRESENT column.

PRESENT   PAST

Press

Happen

Hear

Filling

Arrive

Crossword 1

Name..

<ACROSS>
- 3 present tense for frightened
- 5 past tense for meeting
- 6 past tense for pleasing
- 9 past tense for going

<DOWN>
- 1 present tense for crept
- 2 present tense for driving
- 4 past tense for taking
- 7 past tense for living
- 8 past tense for stop

Tutor Notes Session Two

Starter
You will probably need to explain the past progressive form. The past progressive describes an action that was in progress at a specific time in the past. Students need to understand that the past progressive form serves two functions; namely:

- the description of an action that was started in the past and was interrupted by a second action,
- the description of two simultaneous actions in the past.

Use the powerpoint supplied for this session.

Main Activity
Read through the worksheets with the students and ensure they understand what is required of them. We suggest you ask them to complete the first two worksheets in pairs and compare their answers as they go. This should encourage them to be very self-aware of their own sentence construction.

Plenary
Ask them to complete S1W3 on their own and then compare their answers with their neighbour.

The worksheets on page 19 and 20 are provided as extra learning opportunities for your students. They will require professional judgement on your part as to their suitability for your students.

<u>Warning</u>
<u>Make sure you read Even More on the Past Progressive Form first. We were asked to produce something that would interest young adults, however this may be unsuitable for your students.</u>

© 2018 Lawler Education Teachers may copy these pages for use in their own school.

Session Two Worksheet 1   **Name**..............................

Fill in the correct form of the past progressive in these sentences.

1   What .... the teacher .... at exactly 12 noon yesterday ?   (do)

2   Fred and Natalie .... to the shop when it .... to rain. (walk/start)

3   When Jack .... the house, Charlotte was .... to see him. (enter/delight)

4   Maria .... on the phone when the doorbell .... (talk/ring)

5   Kiku .... her friend when her manager .... into the office. (email/walk)

6   Graham .... on the M6 when the crash .... (drive/happen)

7   Judith .... the car when the delivery .... (wash/arrive)

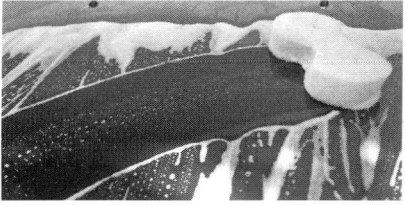

8   Carolyn .... to read the book when she .... Matt arrive from work. (start/hear)

9   Birju and her husband .... for the bus then .... to walk. (wait/decide)

10   The aircraft .... to the start of the runway, ready for take-off. (taxi)

Session Two Worksheet 2 Name..................................

You need to put the verbs in brackets into the gap and form negative sentences in the past progressive form. You can use the long or the short form. Look at the example to see what you need to do.

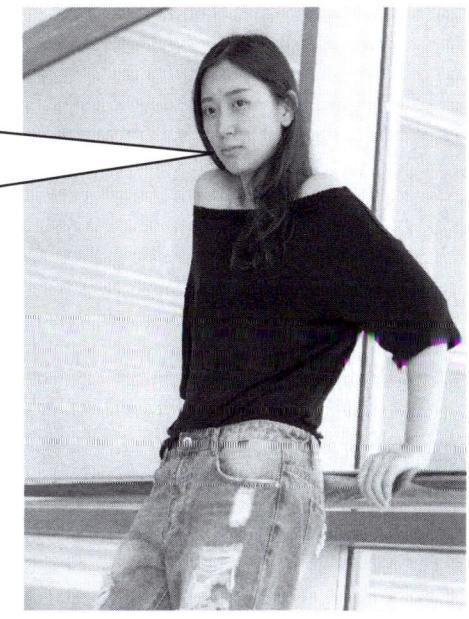

Example

Manisha _____ tennis. (not/to play)

Manisha **was not** playing tennis.

Manisha **wasn't** playing tennis.

1   She _____ a hamburger. (not/ to eat)

2   They _____ to the cinema. (not/to go)

3   Damien _____ the tv news. (not/ to watch)

4   Rob _____ cricket on Sunday. (not/ to play)

5   Martin _____ on the computer. (not/ to work)

6   Carol _____ on Saturday. (not/ to bake)

7   Niomi _____ her homework for school. (not/ to complete)

8   Sarah and Gary _____ enough vegetables this week. (not/ to buy)

9   Nisha _____ eat breakfast at home, she bought it on the way to work. (not/ to eat)

10 Bharat _____ with the company, he is starting his own business. (not/ to stay)

Session Two Worksheet 3   Name ....

This worksheet is more practice on the past progressive form. You do need to practise and make sure you are clear how to form these sentences.
Try making sentences of your own and changing them to the past progressive form.

1   When she was _____ an email the phone _____. (to write/ring)

2   Hema was _____ the exam when the bell _____ (to finish/ring)

3   Nav was _____ the car when the postman _____. (to wash/ to arrive)

4   They were _____ the bill while I was waiting to be _____. (to pay/seat)

5   Mary was _____ because Nigel had _____ her obvious lies. (to worry/to say)

6   Alan and Kevin were _____ for her when the plane _____. (to wait/to land)

7   *Celtic Thunder* were _____ at the theatre, we _____ the show. (to play/ to enjoy)

8   It was early in the morning and that idiot was _____ again. (to shout)

9   Wasn't Fred _____ at the bus stop when you drove past ?   (to wait)

10 Were you _____ on the laptop when the power went off ? (to work)

More on the Past Progressive Form   Name.....................................

1. When I phoned Ron he _____ the evening meal for himself and Julie.
   (cook)

2. Yesterday at six in the evening I_____ the evening news.
   (watch)

3. The children ____ in the garden when it started to rain
   (play)

4. I _____ the piano when Jane arrived.
   (practise)

5. They _____ all day.
   (not cycle)

6. While Bharat _____ in his computer studio, his friends _____ cards.
   (work)   (play)

7. Jay tried to tell them the truth but they _____
   (not/listen)

8. Mary and Roshni _____ through the movie eating chocolates.
   (sit)

Even More on the Past Progressive Form   Name……………………………………

Fill in the blanks with the correct word.

Sullivan's mood was the same as his coat, black and filthy, so when the phone _____ (ring) as he was about to leave the office he _____ (groan). He _____ (bend) his six foot three frame and cursed inwardly as the sciatica _____ (race) down his right leg.

He said ' John Sullivan'.

Sullivan heard a female voice came back, ' Dad it's Sarah'.

For the first time that day, Sullivan _____ (smile) at the sound of his daughter's voice.

'Hi, you ok ?'

'No dad, you have to listen to this man, he has got me and will not let me go unless you do as he says. Dad I'm _____ (scare)'.

A man's voice came on the line, ' Mr Sullivan..' it was a British accent _____ (think) Sullivan. Sullivan _____ (say) nothing. The voice _____ (continue), ' My name, shall we say is Mr Smith. I have a job for you Mr Sullivan and you will do it or you will never see Sarah again.'

Fear _____ (knot) in Sullivan's stomach. The voice _____ (continue), ' I need you to kill someone,.'

Sullivan said 'You're mad.'

'Quite possibly', said Mr Smith ' but you are an ex-soldier and _____ (serve) in Afghanistan so this should be quite easy for you'.

Sullivan immediately knew he was _____ (deal) with a sociopath. Mr Smith said ' Get the police _____ (involve), Sarah dies' The phone went dead.

Tutor Notes Session Three

Starter

Introduce the students to upspeak which is also called high rising terminal, uptalk, rising inflection, moronic interrogative or high rising intonation.

This is a useful video on Youtube but will need your professional judgement as to the suitability for your students.
https://www.youtube.com/watch?v=q3o0jz2ocCw

The purpose of this starter is to draw their attention to the fact that emphasis at the end of a statement can be used as a question and/or an exclamation. Take for example the statement 'really'. Ask students to put a question mark or an exclamation mark at the end and then pronounce it, to see the effect.

Main Activity

Read through S3 W1 and S3 W2 and ask the students to work through it. Then ask them to work through S3W3 in silence.

Plenary

Ask them to audio record their answers to S3W3 and play them to the rest fo the group. You should find there are some differences.

Session Three Worksheet 1   Name...

We use capital letters to begin a new sentence.
We also use capital letters for proper nouns, for example names of people, places, books and titles of films.
Can you think of any proper nouns where you need a capital letter ?

Sentences end with full stops. In the United States full stops are called periods. So you may hear someone use the word period for a full stop, it still shows the sentence end.

Look at this paragraph.   Re-write it in the space below with the correct punctuation.

martin was 34 years old and felt 54 to say he was seriously tired would be an under-statement he was exhausted it all began when his wife sally urged him to buy a business she saw it as a way of making money very quickly the problem was neither martin or sally had ever run a business before so buying a chip van was not the best decision for them   running a business is hard work   in business books they talk about working on the business as well as working in the business this means understanding business processes and being able to manage them well this was an area that martin has struggled with after all changing from being a teacher to being a business person is demanding martin has come to realise how demanding it is

_____

_____

_____

_____

_____

_____

Session Three Worksheet 2   **Name** ....

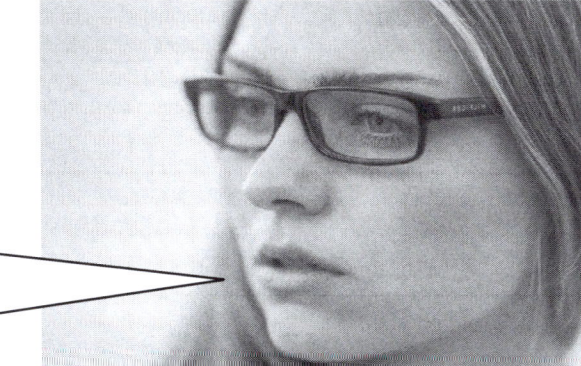

Sentences do not always end in full stops or periods.
Sometimes they can end in exclamation marks or question marks. So what are exclamation and question marks ?

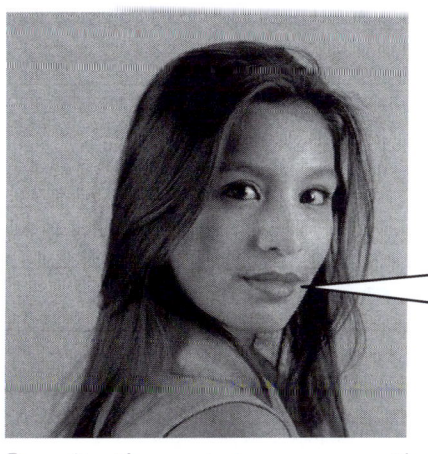

An exclamation mark shows strong feeling in a sentence. Feelings like fear, anger, or love. A question mark shows a question has been asked.

Rewrite these sentences as active sentences with exclamation marks.

Example: John tells Sundar that Sundar did a great job.
Answer : John said, ' That was a great job Sundar!'

1   Mary is asking the way to the library.

_____

2   Afya is telling Gharam that she is excited because Jad is coming to see her.

_____

3   Mair is talking to Gethin on the phone and asking when he will be home.

_____

4   Jan is pleased that Wei is flying in tomorrow.

_____

Session Three Worksheet 3 Name ....

Rewrite the piece below and put in the punctuation. Remember capital letters, full stops, question marks and exclamation marks!
Don't forget commas, where there are lists, you need commas. Good luck!

he sat there with his jaw firmly set i had seen that look before and there was no moving him but dad i said and before i could say anymore he said no i looked around the lounge of his and my mother helens comfortable home in aberford, where they had made their retirement it was lovely but a far cry from the start he had in ireland, living in a 2 bedroomed cottage with no gas water electricity at eighty years old he still had a glorious, distinguished white head of hair, unlike me with my bald head but the one thing he had passed onto me his youngest son was the same streak of stubbornness because there was no way I was going to give in either but I was weakening, and he saw it feebly i said youve got to i do not have to at all but i cant tell it i said i havent lived it its your story how you left ireland and came to Wales and all of the different people you met and what you got up to he looked at me and asked you seriously expect me to write that

Tutor Notes Session Four

Starter

We suggest that you start this session with a query regarding how much the students know about apostrophes.

It is important that they understand that there are two main rules in English regarding the use of the apostrophe:
- they are used to denote ownership of possessions: eg Mark's car.
- they are used to denote a missing letter or letters, for example : I can't instead of I cannot.

Main Activity

Read through worksheet 1 and 2 with the students and ask them to complete them indicually

Plenary

Ask them to complete the wordsearch or if they need extra pratice you have worksheets 3 and 4.

Session Four Worksheet 1   Name ....

Apostrophes are important. The purpose of this worksheet is to learn the first of the two main rules . It is important to put the effort in here and make sure you are clear how they work.

The first rule is that apostrophes are used to show ownership.
Here you put the apostrophe after the word and then add an s, so Mark's Car means the car that belongs to Mark.

Rewrite the sentences and put the apostrophe in the correct place to show ownership.

1   Colins house is on Arkwright Avenue.

2   The dogs bone is smelly.

3   My daughter went to her friend Janes house to do her homework.

4   Nishas cooking was awesome, we really enjoyed the meal at her flat.

5   Jans new shoes are red.

Session Four Worksheet 2

Name......................................

More on Apostrophes

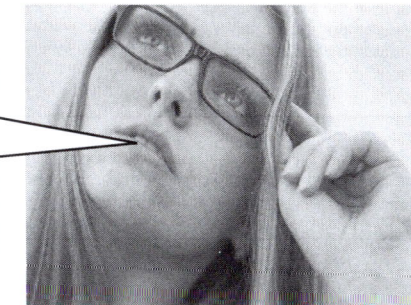

The second rule is that apostrophes are used to show contractions
A contraction means where we miss out letters and join words, for instance do not becomes don't, cannot becomes can't.

Rewrite these sentences with contractions

1 Who is at the door ?

_____

2 You are not supposed to be here.

_____

3 They are not invited to my party.

_____

4 I cannot drive any faster, it is against the law.

_____

5 The meeting is at nine o'clock, do not be late.

_____

Session Four Worksheet 3 Name...

Even More Apostrophes

The purpose behind this worksheet is to combine the two rules we have used so far. These sentences will need to have both possession and contractions.

Rewrite these sentences showing possession and contractions.

1   Matt does not want to borrow Marys book

2   I did not say it was Nishas, Nishas car was not dirty, she washes it every Sunday

3   Hemas birthday was yesterday, and she was not happy to have to work.

4   Judiths plants were not watered when she was away; she was not impressed with Stuart

5   Martins computer was delivered at 3pm, but he was not in to receive it.

Session Four Worksheet 4
Yet even More on Apostrophes

Name..

On this worksheet you need to complete each sentence with two contractions that make sense.

1   Sally _____ found your keys yet but _____ keep looking.

2   Hassan said _____ put the dinner in the oven and _____ be ready in about forty minutes.

3   _____ all having such great time on holiday that we _____ want to leave and come home.

4   I _____ believe that Sonia says _____ going scuba diving.

5   _____ on his way and I think _____ be here in about an hour.

Word Search

Name..

a	r	e	n	'	t	h	e	'	s	w	h	o	'	s
s	h	o	u	l	d	n	'	t	j	d	t	d	v	t
x	q	q	n	t	t	y	w	m	w	o	h	j	c	x
v	l	c	w	t	b	k	e	y	s	n	e	b	e	f
d	p	d	q	t	p	r	r	t	s	'	y	x	r	h
c	v	j	z	h	u	f	e	e	n	t	'	k	l	e
o	p	f	y	e	e	j	n	h	'	d	l	f	'	b
u	u	t	w	y	a	l	'	l	t	u	l	l	l	m
l	t	g	o	'	c	x	t	s	h	e	'	s	l	x
d	w	b	m	r	q	t	t	g	x	u	f	o	b	n
n	u	s	a	e	t	o	x	w	u	h	k	m	b	q
'	d	i	d	n	'	t	a	t	t	f	e	b	r	a
t	i	s	u	l	d	o	e	s	n	'	t	z	q	h
m	w	c	c	h	e	'	l	l	d	d	x	i	j	v
b	v	g	x	g	h	f	f	w	w	x	v	p	b	e

Look for the contractions of these

do not
I will
he will
did not
could not
she is
he is
they are
they will
was not
were not
does not
should not
are not
who is

© 2018 Lawler Education. Teachers may copy these pages for use in their own school.

Answers

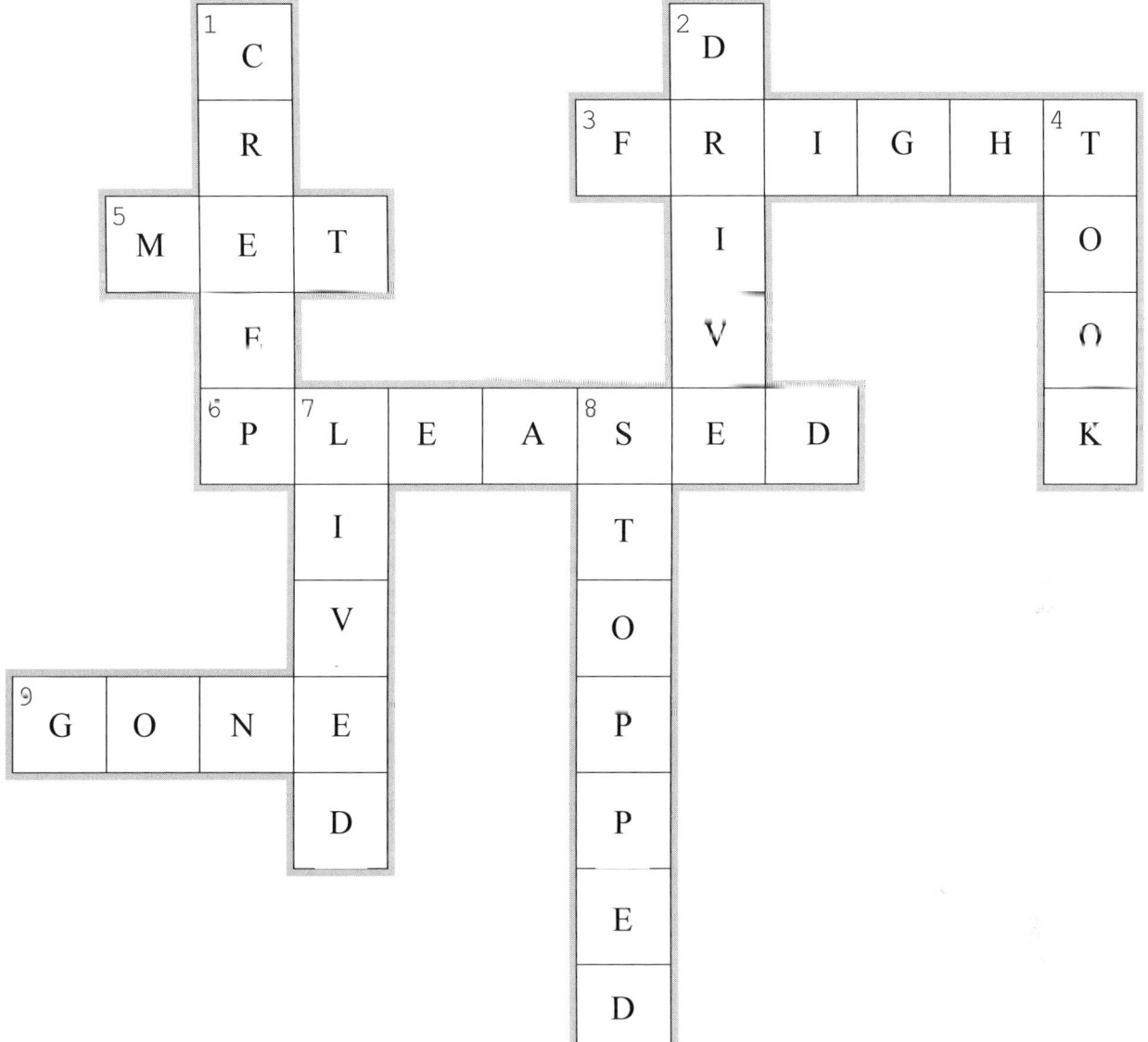

Session One Worksheet 1   Using the Verb 'To be'. p8

1) I **am** hungry.
2) I **am** late.
3) I **am** happy.
4) I **am** tired.
5) We **are** early.
6) We **are** busy.
7) He **is** interesting.
8) She **is** fun.
9) Kevin **is** happy.
10) Sally and Claire **are** my friends.
11) Nisha **is** watching tv.
12) The hammer drill **is** new.
13) The students **are** laughing.
14) The test **is** hard.
15) Manisha is cooking dinner.

Session One Worksheet 1b p9

Aiko **is** starting a job in London next week. She **will** be working for a major media company. Her job involves meeting clients and designing adverts **to be** on the radio. She **had** to learn a lot about British commercial radio because it **really** is so different to the radio she **was** used to back in Japan. Living **in** London is exciting for young people because there **is** so much happening. London **has** top premier football teams and great West End shows, wow life **is** exciting.

Kiku **was** a student at Derwen College until last year. Then she left **to** become a trainee manager at a gardening nursery. She **is** now studying management as part of her training. She hopes, **in** the future, to study for a high management qualification called an M.B.A. Kiku said, ' If I **work** part-time and **study** part-time I can combine the best of both worlds.'
The future **is** going to be hard **work** but **it** will be exciting!'

Jayne **was** delighted to receive her three puppies from her husband. The puppies were to mark thirty years of marriage. Jayne said ' my husband Jacob thought it would be nice to have a pup for each
decade'. Jayne **met** Jacob by chance, when they both worked for a large health company. They **are** both dentists and both **work** for the same dental practice in Chester.
The puppies **are** looked after during the day by a kennel maid who **feeds, walks** and **plays** with them so they **are** content. Even so, every night when Jayne and Jacob **come** home from work, the puppies are so **excited** to see them and run around like crazy for about ten minutes. It **is** great that they are so happy!

Cathy and Jim **are** a new kind of worker. They **are** called ' digital nomads'. That means they work on laptops and **can** work from anywhere in the world. This **is** great for young people because it means they **can** provide services online that someone else, anywhere else, **can** buy. Cathy and Jim write code, and **they** can work anywhere where there **is** access to the internet.
They have both **learned** a lot and **have** visited a lot of countries; what a fantastic life!

Answers

Session One Worksheet 2 p10

Detective Inspector John Mundela **has** a secret. By day he **is** a hard working police officer in Chester but at night he **has** a different job. John Mundela had developed a new **part**-time lucrative career as a novelist. This **means** he writes books to **entertain** his readers.

The real point **is** that none of his fellow workers know that he **is** the famous novelist Dax Brydon. Lots of other **police** officers have commented on how realistic the **Dax** Brydon stories are but no-one has ever thought to **ask** who writes them and John Mundela has never said.

He **writes** under a pseudonym. This **is** a false name and it **means** he can have a private life and make money but why does he carry on **working** as a police officer ?

The real reason is that **writing** novels is not that well paid. People do it for the love of it and if they **happen** to make a lot of money well that is great but the vast majority simply do not **make** a great deal of money.

This has never **been** a problem for Mundela. He enjoys the **writing** process of making a novel, the most. Plotting means working out 'whodunnit' or who **is** the killer. Then the **author** has to lay a series of clues in the story to tempt the reader and the game is that the **reader** has to try and work it out before the end of the book. Millions of people love **books** like this, not because they are gruesome stories of murder but because they are **puzzles** and who does not like a good puzzle ? This is also the reason that there are so many **cop** shows on tv.

Mundela's detective **is** called Jack Caeser. This **is** a great name for a cop and one that **has proven** to be very **popular** with the public. His last novel was called Caeser's Palace and was set in the police station in Chester. People who **read** the book were amazed at how **accurate** the descriptions were but they simply did not realise that the author was **working** in the building most days of the week.

Mundela **started** writing, ' The door handle **moved** and the door **opened** slowly. Detective Inspector Jack Caeser **walked** into the room.'

Session One Worksheet 3 p11
More Tenses Practice

1. My sister **takes** the dog for a walk every afternoon.

2. We are **going** to Chester tomorrow.

3. Jan was **pleased** to see Graham after so many years, they were friends in college.

4. We **have lived** here for twelve years.

5. Mark **was having** his lunch in the staff restaurant when I saw him.

6. We **have never** seen her before.

7. I **met** the solicitor last week.

8. She said she will **see** you tomorrow.

© 2018 Lawler Education Teachers may copy these pages for use in their own school.

Session One Worksheet 4
Even More Tenses Practice p12

Mark and Sarah were **driving** along the M6 to visit friends in the midlands when they realised they needed to stop for petrol.

They **stopped** at a service station and everything **seemed** fine. Mark was **filling** the car when he **heard** a noise. He **saw** two masked men with guns **surrounding** a security van that had **arrived** to collect the money from the petrol station.

Mark left the petrol pump holster in the tank and **crept** along the side of the car to the passenger door. He **said** to Sarah 'slide down onto the floor and stay there'. Sarah just **nodded**. She was very **frightened** and was not going to argue. Mark then **hid** behind the petrol pump and got his phone. He **dialled** 999 but when the operator **answered**, he couldn't **speak**. So he waited and then **pressed** 55. This is a way of **telling** the operator that to speak or make a noise is **dangerous.**

Thankfully after about 5 minutes police cars **arrived** and the criminals were **arrested.**

Mark and Sarah **gave** their details to the police and were soon on their way. Their friends were **amazed** when they **heard** what **happened.**

Session One Worksheet 5
Matching p13
Press **PRESSED**
Happen **HAPPENED**
Hear **HEARD**
Filling **FILLED**
Arrive **ARRIVED**

Session Two Worksheet 1 p16
1   What **DID** the teacher **DO** at exactly 12 noon yesterday ?
2   Fred and Natalie **WERE WALKING** to the shop when it **STARTED** to rain.
3   When Jack **ENTERED** the house, Charlotte was **DELIGHTED** to see him.
4   Maria **WAS TALKING** on the phone when the doorbell **RANG.**
5   Kiku **WAS EMAILING** her friend when her manager **WALKED** into the office.
6   Graham **WAS DRIVING** on the M6 when the crash **HAPPENED.**
7   Judith **WAS WASHING** the car when the delivery **ARRIVED**.
8   Carolyn **WAS STARTING** to read the book when she **HEARD** Matt arrive from work.
9   Birju and her husband **WAITED** for the bus then **DECIDED** to walk.
10   The aircraft **TAXIED** to the start of the runway, ready for take off.

Session Two Worksheet 2 p17
1   She **WASN'T EATING** a hamburger.
2   They **DIDN'T GO** to the cinema.
3   Damien **DIDN'T WATCH** the tv news.
4   Rob **DIDN'T PLAY** cricket on Sunday.
5   Martin **DIDN'T WORK** on the computer.
6   Carol **DIDN'T BAKE** on Saturday.
7   Niomi **DIDN'T COMPLETE** her homework for school.
8   Sarah and Gary **DIDN'T BUY** enough vegetables this week.
9   Nisha **DIDN'T EAT** eat breakfast at home, she bought it on the way to work.
10   Bharat **DIDN'T STAY** with the company, he is starting his own business.

Session Two Worksheet 3 P 18
1   When she was **WRITING** an email the phone **RANG**.
2   Hema was **FINISHING** the exam when the bell **RANG.**
3   Nav was **WASHING** the car when the postman **ARRIVED.**
4   They were **PAYING** the bill while I was waiting to be **SEATED**.
5   Mary was **WORRIED** because Nigel had **TOLD** her obvious lies.
6   Alan and Kevin were **WAITING** for her when the plane **LANDED**.
7   *Celtic Thunder* were **PLAYING** at the theatre, we **ENJOYED** the show.
8   It was early in the morning and that idiot was **SHOUTING** again.
9   Wasn't Fred **WAITING** at the bus stop when you drove past ?
10   Were you **WORKING** on the laptop when the power went off ?

More on the past progressive form p 19
1. When I phoned Ron he **WAS PREPARING** the evening meal for himself and Julie.
2. Yesterday at six in the evening I **WATCHED** the evening news.
3. The children **PLAYED** in the garden when it started to rain.
4. I **WAS PRACTISING** the piano when Jane arrived.
5. They **DIDN'T CYCLE** all day.
6. While Bharat **WORKED** in his computer studio, his friends **PLAYED** cards.
7. Jay tried to tell them the truth but they WOULDN'T LISTEN.
8. Mary and Roshni **SAT** through the movie eating chocolates.

Even More on the Past progressive Form p20

Sullivan's mood was the same as his coat, black and filthy, so when the phone **RANG** as he was about to leave the office he **GROANED**. He **BENT** his six foot three frame and cursed inwardly as the sciatica **RACED** down his right leg.

He said ' John Sullivan'.

Sullivan heard a female voice came back, ' Dad it's Sarah'

For the first time that day, Sullivan **SMILED** at the sound of his daughter's voice.

'Hi, you ok ?'

'No dad, you have to listen to this man, he has got me and will not let me go unless you do as he says. Dad I'm **SCARED**'. A man's voice came on the line, ' Mr Sullivan..' it was a British accent **THOUGHT** Sullivan. Sullivan **SAID** nothing. The voice **CONTINUED**, ' My name, shall we say is Mr Smith. I have a job for you Mr Sullivan and you will do it or you will never see Sarah again.'

Fear **KNOTTED** in Sullivan's stomach. The voice **CONTINUED,** ' I need you to kill someone,.'

Sullivan said 'You're mad.'

'Quite possibly', said Mr Smith ' but you are an ex-soldier and **SERVED** in Afghanistan so this should be quite easy for you'. Sullivan immediately knew he was **DEALING** with a sociopath. Mr Smith said ' Get the police **INVOLVED,** Sarah dies' The phone went dead.

Session Three Worksheet 1 p20

Martin was 34 years old and felt 54. To say he was seriously tired would be an under-statement, he was exhausted. It all began when his wife sally urged him to buy a business; she saw it as a way of making money very quickly. The problem was neither Martin or Sally had ever run a business before, so buying a chip van was not the best decision for them. Running a business is hard work. In business books they talk about working on the business as well as working in the business. This means understanding business processes and being able to manage them well. This was an area that Martin has struggled with, after all changing from being a teacher to being a business person is demanding. Martin has come to realise how demanding it is.

Session Three Worksheet 2 p23

1. Mary asked, ' Is this the way to the library?'

2. Afya said 'Gharam, Jad is coming to see me.'

3. Mair asked 'Gethin when will you be home ?'

4. Jan was pleased when she said ' Wei is flying in tomorrow'.

Session Three Worksheet 3

He sat there with his jaw firmly set, I had seen that look before and there was no moving him.

'But dad', I said and before I could say anymore, he said 'no'. I looked around the lounge of his and my mother Helen's comfortable home in Aberford, where they had made their retirement. It was lovely, but a far cry from the start he had in Ireland, living in a 2 bedroomed cottage with no gas water electricity. At eighty years old he still had a glorious, distinguished white head of hair; unlike me with my bald head. But the one thing he had passed onto me, his youngest son, was the same streak of stubbornness, because there was no way I was going to give in either, but I was weakening, and he saw it. Feebly I said ' you've got to'.

' I do not have to at all.'

' But I cant tell it, ' I said. I haven't lived it, it's your story. How you left ireland and came to Wales and all of the different people you met and what you got up to. He looked at me and asked ' you seriously expect me to write that ?'

Session Four Worksheet 1

1. Colin's house is on Arkwright Avenue.
2. The dog's bone is smelly.
3. My daughter went to her friend Jane's house to do her homework.
4. Nisha's coooking was awesome, we really enjoyed the meal at her flat.
5. Jan's new shoes are red.

Session Four Worksheet 2 p27
More on Apostrophes

1. **Who's** at the door ?
2. **You're** not supposed to be here.
3. **They're** not invited to my party.
4. I **can't** drive any faster, it is against the law.
5. The meeting is at nine o'clock, **don't** be late.

Session Four Worksheet 3
Even More on Apostrophes

1. Matt **doesn't** want to borrow Marys book.
2. I **didn't** say it was **Nisha's**, **Nisha's** car **wasn't** dirty, she washes it every Sunday.
3. **Hema's** birthday was yesterday and she **wasn't** happy to have to work.
4. **Judith's** plants were not watered when she was away, she **wasn't** impressed with Stuart.
5. **Martin's** computer was delivered at 3pm but he **wasn't** in to receive it.

Session Four Worksheet 4
Yet Even More on Apostrophes

1. Sally **hasn't** found your keys yet but **she'll** keep looking.
2. Hassan said **he'll** put the dinner in the oven and **it'll** be ready in about forty minutes.
3. **We're** all having such great time on holiday that we **don't** want to leave and come home.
4. I **can't** believe that Sonia says **she's** going scuba diving.
5. **He's** on his way and I think **he'll** be here in about an hour.

Wordsearch p30 Answers

a	r	e	n	'	t	h	e	'	s	w	h	o	'	s
s	h	o	u	l	d	n	'	t	j	d	t	d	v	t
x	q	q	n	t	t	y	w	m	w	o	h	j	c	x
v	l	c	w	t	b	k	e	y	s	n	e	b	e	f
d	n	a	y	l	p	r	r	t	s	'	y	x	i	h
c	v	j	z	h	u	f	e	c	n	t	'	k	l	e
o	p	f	y	e	e	j	n	h	'	d	l	f	'	b
u	u	t	w	y	a	l	'	l	t	u	l	l	l	m
l	t	g	o	'	c	x	t	s	h	e	'	s	l	x
d	w	b	m	r	q	t	t	g	x	u	f	o	b	n
n	u	s	a	e	t	o	x	w	u	h	k	m	b	q
'	d	i	d	n	'	t	a	t	t	f	e	b	r	a
t	i	s	u	l	d	o	e	s	n	'	t	z	q	h
m	w	c	c	h	e	'	l	l	d	d	x	i	j	v
b	v	g	x	g	h	f	t	w	w	x	v	p	b	e

Interactive White Board Activities 1

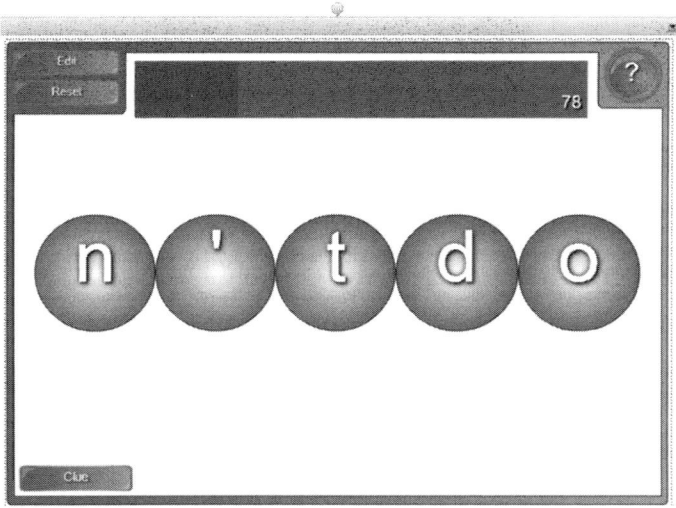

This is an anagram game of contractions. There are three versions on the disc associated with this book, slow, medium and fast. The student has to move the balls by hand on the screen and make the contraction. If they need it, they can press the clue on the bottom left of the screen.

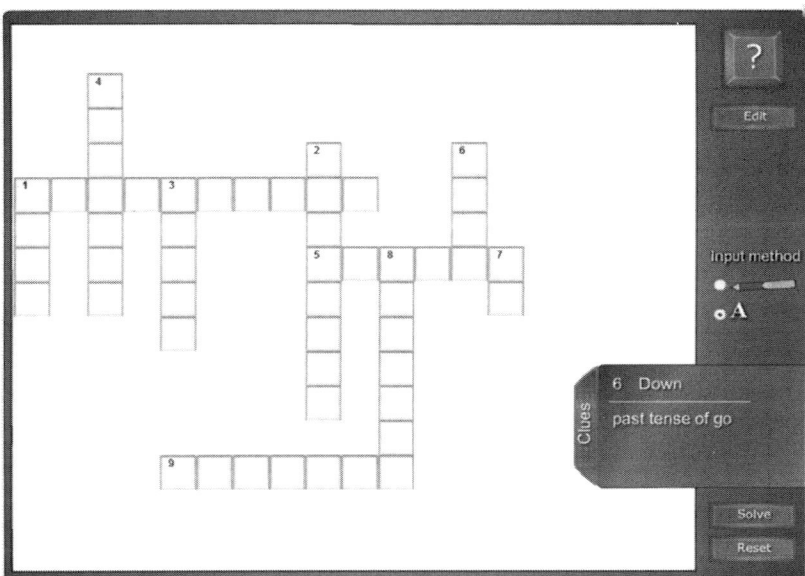

This is a crossword program. Make sure the students have the clue tagged drawn out from the left hand side so that they can read the clue.
The words and clues are as follows:

Do	Make something happen
Pleased	past tense of please
Gone	past tense of go
Stopped	Past tense of stop
Located	Discovered an exact place or position.
Measured	Past tense of to apply a standard scale or measuring device to something.
Solved	Police say this when they have worked out who the guilty person is
Translated	Past tense for changing words from one language to another.
Took	Past tense of take.
Spoke	Past tense of speak

Interactive White Board Activities 2

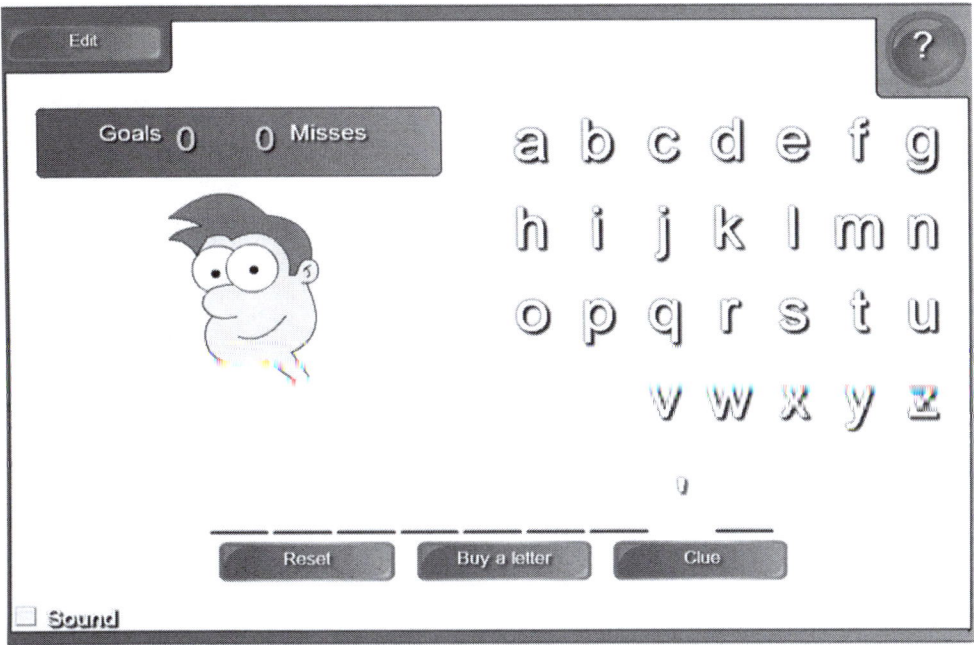

This is tomato splat. Students have to spell out the words to get the splat to work. The words and clues are:

Took	past tense of take
Going	present tense equivalent to present tense of gone.
Pleased	past tense of please
Don't	contraction of do not
Saw	past tense of see
Shouldn't	contraction of should not
Would've	contraction of would have
Gave	past tense of give
Amazed	past tense of amaze
Can't	contraction of can not

Notice on the bottom left there is a sound button (if you want it).

Students need to click on the clue button and then spell the required word. Unfortunately the answer of the contractions do not show the apostrophe in this software so please ensure students are aware that there is a need for an apostrophe.

Will you join our team of authors?

We are looking for new authors in basic skills and level 1/2 apprenticeship training.

If you are teaching in primary, secondary or F. E. or training in industry and would like to be an author, do get in touch: info@graham-lawler.com